From Success to SIGNIFICANCE

Advance Praise For Kris' Message

"This Journey that Kris Mathis has been on has been an experience of unique test and triumphs. This book will unveil the genius that lives inside him as a young man being born with the odds against him. The message this book entails is how all of us can still achieve our dreams even with all the odds against us. Kris is truly one who has lived his testimony and bounced back and beat the odds of just settling for the status quo. He will inspire you and show you how important it is to see things with a fresh set of eyes. Get ready for your genius to arise in your family, business and in your creativity."

—**John L. Evans, Author of**
It's Not My Fault, But It Is My Time!

"In From Success to Significance, *Kris Mathis gives hope to all of us who struggle with believing in the possibilities of who we can be. He teaches us through living his own dream and sharing the tools we need to accomplish our dreams. Then, he helps us to discover significance in our life through helping others. Kris gives us the steps to living our dream; and he helps us discover how to unlock the barriers of humiliation, stress and discouragement in others who have forgotten they have a special personal value to share."*

—**Jack Greenfield,**
President/CEO of Arbor Circle Corp.

"Kris, I am inspired by your speech, life struggle, and the success that has come through you overcoming your obstacles. You have motivated me to send my fears packing. I thank God Almighty for your life."

—Grace Yoka, Founder of Rusinga Mwisho Mother and Child, Vienna, Austria

"Kris, I am truly inspired by how you turned your life's challenges into a source of energy to help yourself and others. As you share your own past pain, you allow others to connect with you and ultimately choose a better life for themselves and those around them. Keep up the great work Kris, and if in the future I can help bring more opportunities your way, I will be sure to do so.

All the best, Katy."

—Katy D. Jacks, Owner/Partner, N2R Media, Liverpool, U.K.

"Kris has been tried in ways few of us ever are, and is living a productive life nonetheless. He is in a good position to speak about motivation. He is bright, motivated to contribute his talents to the community, and energetic. He is a terrific speaker and moved us considerably."

—Michael Williams Ph.D., Professor Emeritus, Aquinas College

From Success to
SIGNIFICANCE

The 8 Keys to Achieving any Goal or Dream

KRIS MATHIS
with Shannon L. Harris

New York

From Success to SIGNIFICANCE
The 8 Keys to Achieving any Goal or Dream

ISBN 978-1-61448-325-0 paperback
ISBN 978-1-61448-326-7 eBook
Library of Congress Control Number: 2012945359

Morgan James Publishing
The Entrepreneurial Publisher
5 Penn Plaza, 23rd Floor,
New York City, New York 10001
(212) 655-5470 office • (516) 908-4496 fax
www.MorganJamesPublishing.com

KRIS MATHIS
Motivational Speaker & Author

Interior Design by:
Bonnie Bushman
bonnie@caboodlegraphics.com

Habitat
for Humanity®
Peninsula and
Greater Williamsburg
Building Partner

From Success to SIGNIFICANCE

The 8 Keys to Achieving any Goal or Dream

is available at special quantity discounts for bulk purchases for sales promotions, premiums, fundraising, and educational use. Special versions or book excerpts can also be created to fit specific needs.

For more information visit **www.krismathis.com** and email your request or call **616-633-4939**.

DEDICATION

This book is dedicated to my mother Deborah and wife Chawntrell.

To my mother,

I know I have not been the 'perfect son' over the years. I have done things as a youth that I am not proud of. Since then, with the help of those who care about me, I have dedicated my life to becoming the best man, son, husband, and one day father that I can be. I want to say thank you for not giving up on me. Thank you for the sacrifices you made to give us a better life. Thank you for all that you have done to help me reach this dream. This book would not be possible if it were not for your hard work, patience, and love.

To my wife Chawntrell,

You have been my biggest supporter during the preparation of this book. Every challenge that came my way you encouraged me to keep fighting. You have never doubted my dreams or ideas no matter how crazy and farfetched they might be. You believed in me at times when I found it hard to believe in myself. I want to say thank you for your ongoing love, encouragement, and support during the writing of this book.

TABLE OF CONTENTS

AUTHOR'S NOTES

This is a work of nonfiction based on my life experiences. I have rendered the events faithfully and truthfully just as I have recalled them. The 8 key ingredients that are given in this book were created by me and used on my journey to help me reach my dreams. Some names and descriptions of individuals have been changed in order to respect their privacy. The words in this book are told in a way that evokes the real feeling and meaning of what was said and my view of what happened to me. While keeping in mind the true essence of the mood and sprit of those moments that shaped my life.

PREFACE

When I was introduced to Kristofer Mathis at a media conference in 2007, in my mind I was meeting just another person. At the media conference, he shared his story with the public, we shared casual pleasantries and then I kindly excused myself to continue on with my existence. It wasn't until we participated in a training on youth master planning facilitated by National League of Cities in Hampton, Virginia that my initial hollow banter was quickly eclipsed by in-depth conversations about life, liberty and the pursuit of my happiness. These were conversations I didn't intend to have but did; not out of obligation but out of perplexing curiosity of just who this man was that kept challenging me with: "If you could do anything in the world and knew you couldn't fail, what would that be? What are your plans to make that a reality?" Needless to say, from that point on, the conversations multiplied and a friendship developed. I'm honored to have been asked to be a contributor to this project.

Kristofer Mathis is deliberate with his words and genuine in his passion for people to truly reach their potential. His depth of knowledge, intuition and life lessons add credibility to this body of work that has taken a lifetime to write, and rightfully so. Although this book isn't an autobiography, it candidly reveals the drama of life that most would only expose in isolation. Such illuminations don't cripple or embarrass Kristofer, they empower him as they will the reader.

This book, whether read as a narrative or as a manual, is for anyone who's had a dream deferred, a dream delayed, a dream realized or all of the above. Each chapter builds upon the other in a most effective blend of anecdotal passages, inspirational epiphanies and a to-do list that's quite frankly, doable. The skinny of this book: read it and be ready for a transformation. Then, pay it forward with intensity and purpose.

—Shannon L. Harris

B.S. in Journalism, Florida A&M University

Choreographer and Published Author

ACKNOWLEDGMENTS

I would like to personally thank the following people for their contributions to helping me through the process of writing and completing this book:

I would like to start by acknowledging my co-author Shannon L. Harris. Thank you so much for sharing my vision. I appreciate all of your hard work, patience, and commitment to this book. You are a GODSEND.

Thank you Michelle Anzivino for your work and constructive criticism to make this book the best it could possibly be.

Thank you Nick Mayo for your thoughts, ideas and vision for designing the cover of this book. You are very much appreciated!

Thank you to my publisher Morgan James Publishing for believing in my work.

To my mother Deborah Mathis and my mother-in-law Ella Gill. Thank you both for your support, encouragement, and prayers.

I would also like to thank Apostle John Evans, Pastor Gloria Walker, Dickie Jobe, Lynn Heemstra, Matt Casto, Jack Greenfield, Monica Sparks and Dr. Pat Pulliam. You all have something in common, you all believed in me. I want to say thank you to all of you for your prayers, encouraging words, and for giving me a chance to share my message with others. You are very much appreciated!

And last, I would like to thank Charles Mabon, Art Hughes, Tommy Robinson, Dwayne Bowman, Michael Scott, Allen Hight, James Oatis, Kentry Byrd, Derek Wallace, Darrell McCoy, Parker Jacobs, and Daniel Gonzalez. You guys have been true friends from the beginning and more importantly, my brothers. Thank you for all the jokes, laughs, support and encouragement through this process. I genuinely appreciate every single one of you guys.

INTRODUCTION

There I was, again. In a place I thought I had left for good. I had dreams of making it to the top. I left my hometown for bigger and better opportunities in the big city. I was making my own money and moving up in the business world pretty quickly until it all came crashing down, way down. I'm talking about basement-level at my mother's house. It was dark and drafty; muggy and cluttered. It was a place of storage, a place where things got tossed when they were no longer needed nor desired. I blended right in down there because that exterior mirrored my interior. As a young man, this was the epitome of humiliation. So, there I sat on, and stared at, the only two things I owned–my couch and my TV. Zero hope, zero motivation, and a million steps back. I had lost everything I had. To say this was a very stressful and emotional time in my life would be to say there are stars in the night sky - an obvious fact. Nothing mattered anymore. This part of my life I have rarely shared with anyone, until now.

I truly believe I'm a miracle. I'm a walking miracle because I'm not supposed to be living the life I'm living now and I'm not supposed to have endured the extremes of my past. For me to have beaten the odds is incredible! It was hard for me to accept what I've accomplished. It took me a long time just to realize how special this journey has been. I never thought much of it before, but I've realized that I can control my destiny. Now I am ready to share my gift with the world.

I've written this book to share my most personal and private thoughts. I've not written them for the sake of drama, although I've had my fair share, but to illustrate the struggles to success and most importantly, the significance your life should take once you've reached your level of success.

In *From Success to Significance*, you will receive the *8 Key Ingredients* that I have personally used to make my dream a reality. These ingredients have helped me continue to fight for my dreams during my most difficult and challenging times. Through these ingredients I have discovered not only the success that I've worked so hard to achieve, but I've also realized how much more valuable and significant my life has become now that I'm in a position to help others.

I don't know what your goals and dreams are, but I do know this: There is something special about you. There is something great that's been brewing on the inside of you for a long time. You have a gift that needs to be released to the world and I am prepared to help you unleash your true purpose.

Are you willing to take the steps to living your dream?

For you to achieve your dream you will need to be open-minded and have the willpower to follow this "winning recipe" that will give energy to your dreams. Are you ready to begin the journey for your dreams? If so, let's go!

The **8 Key Ingredients** are:

The Reality Check: We All Need One!

You're one of three types of people. Keep reading to make your determination. How you overcome your circumstances equals your level of success or failure.

The Dream: You've Got One—So, It's Possible!

You've had that dream brewing in you for quite some time now. Once you know how to reach your dream, you will begin to see a new path for your life.

It's Possible: Developing The Belief That You Can Live Your Dream!

When you can see the possibilities for your life, your life will take on a whole new meaning!

The Struggle: Struggling is Healthy and Part of the Process!

The road to your dream is filled with road blocks, potholes, detours and rotten eggs for good measure. And with the right coaching and guidance you will learn how to fight your way to the top!

It's Hard: If It Was Easy, We'd All Be Successful!

No one ever said that going after your dream would be painless. You must keep fighting during the good and the bad times. You must not give up when the pressure rises because your dream is strong and can withstand high levels of heat and pressure.

You Must Have Faith: Your Faith has a Huge Appetite!

Faith is the essence, the spice, the zest that holds your dream together. It's the force that's much greater than yours that holds you up when you feel like falling down. Feed the force!

The Victory: 'Tis So Sweet!

Think about how sweet it's going to be and how excited you'll feel when your accomplishments speak for themselves. You're closer than you think!

Significance: 'Tis Sweeter!

You will gain a higher level of self-worth because you chose to share your gifts with others. This will take you to a level of success that most people find hard to reach. The satisfaction of knowing you're making a difference in someone else's life is unparalleled.

While reading through this book, these *8 Key Ingredients* will be the principles that you live by to reach your dream. You will be motivated, inspired, and educated on exactly what you will need to chase and achieve your dream. From there, you can begin to share this with others who have dreams and goals and you will gain something very few "successful people" have ever acquired in life, and that's Significance.

I present to you …

From Success to Significance
The 8 Keys to Achieving any Goal or Dream

Chapter 1

THE REALITY CHECK: WE ALL NEED ONE

"All of us are given a gift in life. The reason most people never succeed is because they are afraid to use it."

Think about what it would feel like if you were to use your gifts and make your dreams a reality. Think about the excitement of being able to do what you love each and every day. Think about the one thing you would do for free and you do it so well, people are paying you to do it.

To make your dream a reality you must have something special within you. This is something that we all possess, but very few of us access. Let me tell you what

I know. I know that you have something special within you! You have a special gift lying dormant deep inside of you that's waiting to be released to the world!

I've learned that living your dreams and reaching your goals are the easy parts. The hardest part is seeing the possibilities for your life and believing that you can do it. It all begins with your belief of what's possible for your life.

Now comes the Reality Check. We all need to conduct a self-assessment of our dreams and goals multiple times throughout our lives. This allows us to evaluate what we've accomplished and what we have yet to accomplish. We must ask ourselves WHO we are, WHERE we are, and WHY we are–so that we can either continue the things we're doing well, be complacent, or change course to get onto the road to success.

I believe there are three types of people in the world. The first are the **Winners**. This group of people is the smallest group of the three. They chant the mantra of, 'It's Possible,' on a daily basis. These people have achieved some of their dreams, reached a few goals, and are now living the life they worked so hard to obtain. They have paid the price of success and understand what it takes to reach their dreams! And because of these strategic beliefs, they now live at a level that most only dream about reaching.

The second group is the **Losers**. This is the largest group of the three and the easiest to join because there are no requirements for membership except for giving up. These are the people who know they are losers and have given up on life. These people have been trampled upon in the race of life because they refused to get up and stand strong in the midst of difficult times. They feel that it's not worth the hassle to fight for their dreams. They have forgotten their own personal value and they have allowed themselves to become comfortable with being a loser. They've made the decision to believe that their current circumstances are the way it is supposed to be; hope is all gone and everything is simply impossible.

Then there's the third group, and this is where I think you come in. These people have great ideas and great dreams, but have not yet found the keys to open them. This group of people go out everyday seeking knowledge and the keys to unlock the door to their dreams. And if they were given an opportunity that would allow them to use their gifts, they would open the door to other opportunities greater than what they could have ever imagined.

These are the people who I call the **Contenders**. These are the winners who have not yet learned how to win. This group of people know that they're winners, but each time they come close to reaching their dream, life seems to get in the way and they come up a little short. They come up short because while driving on the road to success they hit potholes, roadblocks, and detours that they had no idea existed. After hitting a pothole or two, they are now stranded on the side of the road with a flat tire, no experience, and no tools to fix it. They know that if they were given the proper tools, a little coaching, and a touch of guidance they could fix their own flat tire, get back on the road to success, and soon find themselves on amazing journeys that lead them to victory time and time again. These people are willing to go out in stormy weather to get to their dreams! The weather forecast might say, "It's miserable outside, driving is hazardous, stay off the road." But this strange group of people will put on extra clothing to bear the low temperatures and prepare to go out. And before they walk out the front door, they think to themselves, "I'm prepared! The weatherman isn't talking to me."

Contenders are always seeking and searching for new answers that will take their lives to a new level. These people have a deep hunger beyond the average person for a new life. Deep down inside they believe that there's a better way. And they often tell themselves, "I know God has more in store for me! This cannot be it for my life!" These people may have friends and family who look at them weird and don't believe that their dream is worth the trouble and they think they're crazy for doing this!

They say things like, "What's wrong with you? Why can't you just be content with the life that you have? Why do you have to do this? You should give up because it's not worth the hassle!" And then they realize that their friends and family just don't understand. They don't understand that you have a deep hunger that's dying to be fed on the inside of you. Life has thrown everything at you including the kitchen sink and still you continue to push forward because you know that there's got to be a better way. These people are constantly asking questions and feeding their minds with new information. They go through all of this in the pursuit of a new life.

Recap: Key Ingredient #1
THE REALITY CHECK: WE ALL NEED ONE

One of the biggest challenges in life that you will ever face is to go against the beliefs and expectations that your friends and family have for you. Your friends and family may not see your dream and, as hard as it is to admit, some of them will attempt to discourage you from pursuing it. So you must have the courage to go against the grain to pursue what it is that you want in life.

Check all that apply. I am a:

☐ Winner

☐ Loser

☐ Contender

Chapter 2

THE DREAM: YOU'VE GOT ONE SO, IT'S POSSIBLE!

"You're Closer Than You Think"

$\mathcal{M}$any people go through life expecting their dreams to happen for them because they're good people, they go to church, or because they work hard. They attend motivational seminars, read books, and get energized about their goals for 24-48 hours. After that, they sit and they wait. They wait for their dream to magically appear like a rabbit out of a top hat. When the dream doesn't materialize on time or appear according to their specifications, they become frustrated, discouraged, and they give up. An unhealthy and blinding belief system based on status quo, fear, and doubt develops. They live their lives believing that their past and present foreshadows their future impossibilities. If they could only take a moment to believe that their 24-48-hour dream can morph into an amazing future, they will be able to see their desired outcome.

Sometimes when you think about your dream, it's difficult for you to believe you can achieve it. You may get frustrated or even discouraged because of what life is giving you at the moment. You may look at your dream and think that it's such a large mental leap from where you are currently to where you want to be. So for you to look at your dream and say, "I can do it", "I can make it", or "I can have that" may be too much for you to believe. In those times, here is a phrase that you can say to yourself and know to be true. And that phrase is, **It's Possible!**

Even though things aren't working out the way you would like right now–**It's Possible!** Even though your family and friends think you're crazy for chasing this dream–**It's Possible!** Even though you just lost your job, or maybe you were diagnosed with some type of health issue–**It's Still Possible!**

The good news about this is even with all these things happening you're still in the game! You haven't been counted out! And as long as you're in the ring that means all you need is one good punch to win!

The power of dreaming is an interesting subject. I've learned that if you can dream about what it is that you want in life, then it can be done. The beautiful thing about the mind is it can take you to places without you having to leave your home. When you need that short getaway from your reality you can dream and it will take you anywhere you want to go. One reason dreams are so powerful is because they show you the possibilities for your life. It's like watching a movie trailer weeks before the movie comes out. The three-minute trailer is packed with exciting and riveting scenes that make it hard to look away! And because of this trailer, people are excited to see what comes next. This is the same for your life. Albert Einstein once said, "your imagination is your preview to life's coming attractions." Your dreams are a preview of what's to come in your life. If you are willing to dream about what it is that you want, then you will always be excited to see what comes next in your "living movie."

You must take a look at your life's "trailer" and dream day and night to remember the possibilities for yourself. Doing this will strengthen your belief and give you a clear vision of the goal ahead.

I want you to take a moment and go through what I call the **Living Your Dreams Exercise.** This exercise is going to help you create that "trailer" of your life. Get to a quiet room or space for this exercise.

Now I want you to take a moment and envision one dream that you're passionate about.

Now some are going to say, "I'm passionate about more than one thing." Well, like the old saying goes, "The person who chases two rabbits catches none." You can't go in two different directions at once. You must pick one dream and focus on that one first. Once that dream is caught then go after the other. So I want you to pick one dream that you're very passionate about. One dream that you feel you must accomplish in your lifetime. That's the dream I want you to focus on for this exercise.

Ok, ready? Let's go.

1. Relax your body and inhale deeply then exhale deeply. I want you to clear your mind of all thoughts for the next few minutes. Nothing else matters right now except the words on this page and your dream.

2. Remember words have power so answer this aloud. If you could not fail and you were guaranteed success, what's the one dream that

you would accomplish first? Now that you have your dream in your head focus on it.

3. Imagine and say aloud what it will feel like when you achieve this dream. Think about the excitement you will have your first day after achieving this goal. Think about the surreal feeling you will have when this happens. Take a moment and say aloud what this feels like.

4. Look around and tell me who's there to celebrate this moment with you?

5. What city and location is this happening in your dream?

6. Feel the applause from the audience as your name is announced and you walk out on the stage you created. What does that feel like?

7. What product or service do you offer that has the audience so excited?

8. Just stand there. Embrace and appreciate this surreal moment.

9. Imagine the line of people waiting to greet you and thank you for how you've touched their lives. What a feeling!!

10. Think about what you had to go through, the work you put in, and all the sleepless nights you endured to get to this point. Was it worth it?

95% of people after taking this exercise are going to say, **"YES!! IT WAS WORTH IT!!"**

Did you notice that during this exercise I didn't ask you how you were going to get there? Did I ask you if you had everything you needed to make this happen? The answer is no. How you're going to get there and what you need is none of your business!! These are things that really don't matter at this point. What you will realize is the more you envision your dream the more doors will be opened for you. What you need and the path to reach it will appear. All you need to do is visualize you want and the doors will begin to open slowly. Then take a step closer to your dream.

The feeling you had while going through this exercise is the way the **<u>Winners</u>** feel all the time! Everyday they're living their dream! The Winners all started at this same point and because they did this daily along with a few other ingredients, their dream became a reality. They made the decision and had the courage to visualize the next scene of their movie! Nothing else mattered but that!

This 10-minute exercise is very important because it allows you to escape to your "dream place." For 10 minutes you didn't hear that little voice in your head telling you your ideas weren't good enough. You didn't hear the negative friends and family members saying that you're crazy for doing this. Remember, you must do this daily! This exercise will feed your mind the positive beliefs it needs to run strong. You just envisioned a 10-minute preview of your life to be. Get ready!

For years, I thought about pursing my dreams of working in the field of business. I thought maybe one day I'd even author a book about my life and my success. And for years it tugged at my spirit and conversely, it played off my insecurities because I was convinced it was impossible for me. A voice in my head would consistently repeat mantras of self-doubt and fear. "You will never make it! You were born and raised in the inner-city. No one is going to listen to somebody like you! This crazy idea will never happen for you!"

For a long time I believed this to be so. I allowed my environment to dictate to me what my future would be. Growing up, I felt as though I was from the "Land of No Opportunity." As a young man, when I walked out my front door, I didn't see any examples of success, opportunity, or what's possible for my life. I saw prostitutes on the corners in their short skirts and see-through tops. I saw crackheads stumbling up and down my block looking for their next high. And I saw drug dealers selling crack to any corrupted soul who was looking to get a fix. This was my life. There were times when I'd go out to play as a child and I would have to navigate my way through the disgusting used condoms that were deposited along the side of my house. My view of future possibilities was bleak. I innately knew that I had gifts, but I didn't know how to access them. I didn't have dreams of becoming a doctor, lawyer, CEO or even Superman. The examples of success and opportunity were less obvious and more oblivious, especially since I had no friends, no family, nor any other examples of anyone who had ever made it out of my environment.

This gave me the thumbs-up to accept my own excuses and to marinate in my circumstances in which I grown accustomed. And the fear of what life would be like if I left my environment was almost too much for me to think about. Who would I become if I left? Would I have to change who I am to fit in? When I thought about success, I would ask myself these questions. To me the inner-city is similar to a prison without the bars. It holds so many people captive by placing mental shackles on their mind and they give up their rights to see the possibilities for their lives. Just like a prisoner, I did not see the possibilities for my life outside the depressing confines of my environment, so I unconsciously settled into thinking that I should just accept the life that I'd been given. This is how I viewed my life. And living in poverty was not just where I lived, it was who I was. I believed the old saying, "Like father, like son." So, that meant since I had a father who was in and out of jail and on drugs, my "trailer" for my future, if you will, looked more like a straight to DVD tragedy than a chart-topping blockbuster adventure. I never thought that one day I would have the opportunity to change my life forever. I didn't believe in the power of my dreams or the possibility of them becoming true.

Then one day while working in a small deli at our local mall, my life was changed forever!

Recap: Key Ingredient #2
THE DREAM: YOU'VE GOT ONE–SO, IT'S POSSIBLE!

Begin to envision your dream and what it is that you want on a daily basis! This will help you tune out that little voice in your head that always tries to discourage you. It will also show you a preview of your new life to be. Doing this regularly will help you stay focused on the goal ahead. This is a continual reminder to you that you're closer than you think to the dream that you want.

Chapter 3

IT'S POSSIBLE: DEVELOPING THE BELIEF THAT YOU CAN LIVE YOUR DREAM!

"Your life will never be the same after you make the decision that nothing can stop you from reaching your dream."

'*It's* **Possible**' is such a powerful phrase! With this phrase, you can always bring yourself back from troubling and challenging moments. When things aren't going the way you planned them to, say aloud: "**It's Possible!**" Maybe you've had a setback on your journey toward your goals–Lord knows I've had plenty. Say with

17

confidence**, "It's Possible!"** See, one of the beauties in life is that there are always others who have done it before you. Knowing this, you can always look at your dream and know that **It's Possible!** If they can do it, YOU can do it!

May 6, 1954–the belief on the planet was that no human being was physically capable of running one mile in less than four minutes. The world didn't believe it could be done. Then, along came a guy by the name of Roger Bannister. Roger was an athlete who became the first person in the history of the world to run the mile in under four minutes. 46 days later one of his competitors, John Landy, also ran the mile in under four minutes. From then until now, thousands of people have done this "impossible" accomplishment! The only thing that changed since 1954 was that thousands of people believed that it was possible! If Roger can do it, I can do it!

My first obvious *It's Possible* moment came when I was 17-years-old. I was working part-time for a small deli in a shopping mall. Every day at work I would serve soup, sandwiches, and pastries to customers. Although I was only working just a few days a week, I earned enough money to take care of some minor household needs and from time to time, financially help family members. One day I came to work and I was standing at the counter just daydreaming about what it would be like to be "successful;" what it would feel like to be a "somebody." Maybe I would get into some type of business like the people I had seen on BET (Black Entertainment Television). "That would be amazing," I thought to myself.

Across the hall from the deli was a formal wear store. They specialized in tuxedo rentals for weddings, proms, and other black tie events. Whenever things slowed down at the deli, I would lean over the countertop with my head resting in my hands and gaze at the employees across the hall. I would think to myself, "I wonder what it's like working there? Everyone is dressed so nicely!" I wondered what it felt like to go to work all dressed up and go home the way I left, clean. This was unlike my job at the deli where I came home reeking of smoked turkey, smelly cheese and the day's trash. The only time I really got dressed up was when it was time to go to church. Even then, I wore clip-on ties because I never learned to tie a real one and I never wore a suit because I didn't even own one.

As I woke up from this spell of daydreaming, I glanced out into the mall area and I noticed a black man walk into the formal wear store. This man was different from the other customers I saw go into the store. This man didn't stop at the counter at all. He walked passed everyone right into the backroom of the store!

I thought, "Wait a second. What is he doing?" I had been working at the deli about two months or so and I had never seen this guy before! For a split second, I thought he may have worked there but then quickly assumed he was probably just picking up or dropping something off. I continued to observe, hoping my own customers wouldn't distract me from what was going on across the hall. Then, this same guy came out with a nice shirt and tie on, a fresh pair of slacks, and a measuring tape hanging around his neck. Then it hit me, this black guy I just saw walk into the formal wear store was actually an employee!

After seeing this, I almost did not believe it! The place that I conducted hours of surveillance on for months had someone working there that looked like me! Well, at least my height and complexion. My mind began racing with thoughts so fast that I couldn't keep up! I thought to myself, "How did he get hired there? Who is the manager? Are there any other black people working there?" Then I thought, "Maybe I could work there, too." And within a split second of that thought, I heard a voice in my head say, "Kris, you could never do that kind of work. Why waste your time thinking about it? You're from the 'hood' and they don't hire people like you in places like that." After hearing these thoughts, I concluded that I shouldn't waste my time. My "24 hour dream" dissipated. I snapped back to reality by making (what felt like) my billionth turkey on wheat with extra honey mustard.

Even though I was constantly talking myself out of my dream, I still found myself dedicating my lunch hour to watching the employees at the tuxedo store helping customers, joking with one another, and genuinely enjoying what they were doing. For some reason the dream of working there was such a draw. The notion of doing what they did would not leave me alone! I had to at least find out who this man was that I was studying. Now you might think, "Whoa, total stalker." This man was an African-American man like me. Unlike me he looked and acted the part of a professional. I was hooked on what was possible and I wasn't even fully aware of it at the time.

One morning as I was preparing for my shift at the deli, I decided that after work I'd take that journey across the hall and introduce myself to the mystery man. I was convinced that I had nothing to lose because I'd been disappointed so many times in life up to that point, that if I had to deal with another rejection, then it would be a piece of cake. I was so nervous.

I looked like I had just made a sandwich, which, of course, was the case. I mustard up the courage, pun intended; I took a deep breath and began to walk toward the entrance of the formal wear store. As I stepped into the store, a low tone buzzer went off.

A young woman walked out and said, "Hey, how can I help you?"

I answered, "I don't mean to bother you, but I was wondering if you were hiring?"

"You'll want to speak with the manager here. His name is Sean. Why don't you come back tomorrow during the morning and he should be here," the young lady said.

"No problem, I will do that. Thanks for your time."

I then made my way back across the hall to the deli feeling somewhat accomplished because I took a baby step toward my future.

The next day I took another deep breath and began to make my way across the hall again. I walked into the store and like before, the buzzer went off. Out walks a man dressed in a nice shirt, tie, and a full beard.

"Hey, what can I do for you?" he says.

"Are you Sean?" I asked standing there dressed in a pair of jeans that had seen better days, a more than dingy white T-shirt, and a company-issued apron smeared in a dollop of mustard, a dash of mayo, and ground-in breadcrumbs to top it off.

"Yes, I'm Sean. How can I help you?" he said.

"Hey, my name is Kris and I was wondering if you were hiring? I stopped in yesterday and the young lady told me to speak with you."

Sean smiled skeptically at me and said, "Yeah, we're hiring. I've got a few candidates I'm considering, but fill out an application and maybe I'll give you a call if the other applicants aren't the right fit."

Now that may not sound like much to you, but for me that was great news! To be able to apply for this position was a big step for me!

I eagerly said, "Great, I'll take the application and fill it out right now!" Sean handed me an application and I grabbed a seat at the table in the store and began ferociously writing away. Then, all of a sudden, that little voice in my head came back again and said, "You have no experience in this field. What are you doing?" It didn't take me long to complete the application because the fact was, I indeed had no experience in sales and marketing and I had never created a résumé before. So, by not being qualified, I completed the application in no time. I handed it back to Sean and asked, "So when do you think you'll get a chance to look at it?"

"I'm not sure, I'll try and get around to it today," he replied.

I thanked him for his time and began my walk back across the hall feeling equally confident and insecure. I felt confident because I had stepped out of my comfort zone and felt it was a successful move, but I also felt insecure because of my lack of preparation and experience.

I was scheduled to work the next morning and like every other day, my focus was on the store across the hall. The negative voices in my head were a constant, but my desire to be given an opportunity to do something different kept me motivated. I eventually made my way over there for the third time hoping Sean would tell me something positive about the status of my application. But instead, when I walked in and as the buzzer sounded, the African-American man that I had seen through the window of the deli came walking out.

He said, "Hey, how are you?"

"I'm good thanks," I replied. "I was stopping in to see Sean. I turned in an application yesterday and I wanted to see if he had a chance to check it out."

"Oh, you filled out an application here? Cool," he said. I told him my name and he introduced himself as Douglas. Finally, I was able to put a name with the face that I'd seen for the last couple of weeks. He told me a little about his position there and how proud he was to have a hand in helping customers plan their special occasions. I spent my entire break there getting to know Douglas and getting a glimpse of the inner-workings of the store. After our conversation I headed back across the hall to the deli, absolutely elated.

Over the next couple of weeks I stopped into the store almost every day that Douglas worked. I wanted to get to know him and learn more about how he got into his position that he held at the store. I learned that he was from a very poverty-stricken city in Michigan. In the back of my mind I couldn't believe what I was hearing from this guy. Our stories were so similar. The only difference was that he had made it out of that environment and I was still struggling to find my way.

During that same span of time, I saw Sean a few times and each time I saw him I would ask, "So did you get a chance to look at my application?" Every time he would answer the same unenthusiastic way, "Not yet, but I'll get around to it." After a few times of this, I started to get the impression that maybe the voice in my head was right. Maybe Sean felt that I wasn't qualified for the position. Maybe Sean just didn't have it in him to tell me the truth. Maybe he saw the same things I saw in myself—a poor, under-experienced kid from the inner-city. At this point, I began to lose hope in ever working there with Douglas.

Days passed; one shift blended into another. No word from the tuxedo shop. Then one day, just as I started to drift back into daydreaming about the 'if only I could' ideas, I saw Sean start to make his way across the hall towards me.

"Hey Kris, Douglas told me you've been stopping by. Why don't you come and talk with me when you take your break today."

"No problem, I'll be there!"

I wasn't sure where this was going, but I was so excited! Just when I had lost all hope he came to see me! Maybe he changed his mind and saw something special in me, I thought. But once again, that little voice of doubt in my head said, "Or maybe he just wants to tell you that you didn't get the job." Instantly, my balloon filled with excitement became deflated. As I took a deep breath and exhaled, all of my excitement went out with it. I was preparing myself for another disappointment to add to the list.

My 15-minute break arrived and I made my way across the hall to see Sean–expecting the worse. Sean was standing behind the counter as if he had been waiting all day for me to walk in.

"Kris, a few weeks back I told you I had a couple other candidates in mind for the position here, but one of them didn't work out." My heart thumped one strong beat. Then a millisecond later the store buzzer went off. A young couple came into the store and I politely stepped aside. Sean greeted the couple and they mentioned that they were getting married. Sean congratulated them and began to show them different styles in the formal wear catalogues displayed on the table. I stood back watching, just itching to give my two cents even though I didn't know the first thing about formal wear. I pondered my options: I'd either impress Sean with my tenacity and be added to the payroll, immediately, or I would upset Sean and get thrown out of the store, immediately. Either way, what did I have to lose? Then, the phone rang and Sean stepped away from the couple to answer it. While he was on the call, I had the audacity to say, "Don't worry I got this." I was determined to show him my skills!

Standing there in my dingy T-shirt, old jeans, and an apron covered in sandwich condiments, I mustered up the courage (pun intended again) and said to the couple, "How about this look? What do you think of this color? This would be a great fit! And you can put it with this jacket and pant! That would be nice," and so on! The customers were getting so excited over the options I had selected for the biggest day of their lives. Sean hung up the phone, came back, and I stepped out of the way and he finished assisting the couple. I stood there in sheer anticipation, and a bit fearful, as to what Sean would say to me.

After the customers left, Sean said, "Kris, you really impressed me with what you just did. After that, I think you deserve a chance to work here. Are you still interested?" I said, "Of course I am! I would love the opportunity to work here!" And I was added to the payroll, immediately.

Now, let us go back to that dream that I spoke about in the beginning of this chapter. Take a moment and think about your dream and your ability to achieve it. Do you have that little voice in your head saying things like, "You can't do that because you don't have the experience or the education" or "It's never been done, so makes you think you'll be the first?" Maybe you have a friend or family member telling you it will never work and you should just give it up. Here's the reality–God created YOU! He gave YOU the ability to dream in abundance! He allows YOU to see things in your dreams that others cannot see! And if he wanted others to see the vision that YOU have, he would have given it to them as well! Your dream isn't meant for them–it's meant for YOU! The reason why people are so negative and will tell you that your dreams will never work is because they can't see it! So, when you are in the midst of challenging moments, that is when you have to find examples for yourself so that you know–**It's Possible!**

When I went after this job with Douglas and Sean I had no idea how crucial that position would be to my success. No one could have convinced me of it at the time, but I had someone greater pulling me in the direction I was to go.

If it were not for Douglas, whom I am still friends with today, there's a chance I would still be making the sandwich-of-the-day. Had I allowed myself to believe that negative little voice in my head and the naysayer's that spoke against me, I don't know if I would have ever made my way across the hall. Because in listening to them, I wouldn't have believed it was possible for me to do better.

For weeks, I watched and made no effort to apply for the position, but something inside of me wouldn't allow me to sit back and watch anymore. And then when I saw Douglas, I knew it was possible! If he could do it, so could I! Looking back on that experience, I'm proud to say that Sean and Douglas were my mentors. It is critical that you find a mentor or role model who can give you the coaching and guidance that you need to reach the next level. They will serve as an example of what it is you want to accomplish in your life.

Recap: Key Ingredient #3

IT'S POSSIBLE: DEVELOPING THE BELIEF THAT YOU CAN LIVE YOUR DREAM.

First, you must believe that **It's Possible** for you to live your dream! When you look at your dream and it seems too difficult, just say, **"It's Possible!"** When you get frustrated and discouraged because of what life is giving you at the moment, know that **It's Possible** and keep going. Even if you just lost your job, scream aloud, **"It's Possible!"** Remember the power of your words and the importance of saying it aloud.

Every day you must remind yourself, through examples of what's possible, that you have what it takes! **It's Possible** for you to make your dream a reality! And if you continue to believe that **It's Possible** you will amaze yourself by what you can do!

Chapter 4

THE STRUGGLE: STRUGGLING IS HEALTHY AND PART OF THE PROCESS!

"If you are going through some tough times, remember they are not here to stay. They are here to pass. No storm in the history of the world has ever come and stay. Your storm must leave you. I promise you it will end."

I'm very excited for you right now! You're making great progress! If you've made it this far, it's because you've passed the reality check. You've learned how to envision your dream. And now you see the possibilities for your life!

Now, prepare yourself for the fourth ingredient you will need on your journey.

The fourth ingredient is called, **The Struggle.**

During this stage of your journey is when Murphy's Law will kick in. Murphy's Law says, "Anything that can go wrong, will go wrong." Life is going to going to test you, stretch you, and make you uncomfortable. Life will make unexpected things happen. Bad things will happen, things that you won't be prepared for. Life is going to test you to see if you really want this dream to become a reality. Life's goal is to force you to give up on your dream. Life wants to see you quit before you do something great! Life will occasionally ask you things like, "How bad do you want it? How bad do you really want this dream? Let's find out! How about I have your car repossessed? Then your lights at home shut off? Next, your phone will be cut off. Then after that, I'll make sure your home goes into foreclosure. Better yet, let's just have you evicted from your home. Are you employed? Well, not anymore. Now let's see if you still want this dream." This is just a sample of some of the things that can or will happen to you in the fight for your dream!

No one ever told me that one day life would test me with struggles and hardship, especially at such a young age. Life knew even back then that I had something special in me and that I was destined for greatness. And if I ever got the opportunity to show Life, I would do something great with it!

When I look back on my life I now realize that it was necessary that I face these tough times. These times made me appreciate my victory so much more!

The easiest thing I've ever done in my entire life is live my dream. I find it rather easy for me to get up in front of hundreds and thousands of people to discuss overcoming tough times and to illustrate what it takes to truly reach one's goals and dreams. On the other hand, the hardest thing I've ever done in my entire life was believe that I could do this. For a long time I didn't believe it was possible for me to live my dream as a businessman or as a speaker. It took a very long time for me to realize the possibilities for my life. One reason is because I was blinded by my struggle and I allowed my struggle to determine my future.

To believe in yourself is very important when going after your dreams. What's equally important is to realize within yourself that accomplishing your goals and dreams is as necessary as air is to breathing. It must be done to truly be alive.

For years, I didn't believe that I would ever make it this far in life. Due to my background and growing up in the inner-city, I had the belief that very few young black males reached any type of success. According to the Centers for Disease Control and Prevention, "Mortality Among Teenagers," (May 2010), the number one cause of death of black male teenagers between the ages of 12 and 19 is homicide. I assumed that either I'd fall into a statistical category or I'd fulfill the stereotype society places on young black males which is to be incarcerated leaving behind a plethora of children before reaching my potential. When I look back on the last 20 years, all that I've done and all that I've been through, I realized that my life is a miracle! I'm not supposed to be living this life after experiencing the extremes from which I've come. For me to have beaten the odds, it's incredible! It took me a long time just to realize how special this ride has been. I never thought much of it before now.

I didn't believe that one day I would be recognized as a powerful motivational speaker who has helped change the lives of thousands of people. But at several points along my journey, I realized I would never be happy without awakening my dreams and recognizing my true value. To awaken my dreams, I had to believe it was possible and I had to understand that my past experiences–the honorable and the horrible–were necessary occurrences that would help mold me into the man I've become today.

As a child, my life started out very difficult and was filled with challenges and heart breaking experiences. I grew up in a poverty-stricken part of the southeast side of Grand Rapids, Michigan. My father left the family when I was four years old for a life of drugs and crime. Because of my father's choices, my mother was forced into being a single parent. She wasn't prepared for the challenges of raising my sister and I on her own. So, we were forced to move in with my grandparents, who were willing to help us the best they could.

My maternal grandparents lived in a two-level home with six bedrooms. My grandparents had six kids, they were all adults with kids of their own. And even though some of them had moved out, they were all forced to move back at some point due to life's challenges and setbacks. Talk about a crowded house! It seems as though my whole family was going through tough times. There were times when all 20 of us lived together and we had to share everything even though we didn't have much. And when I say everything, I mean from meals, to clothes, to our sleeping arrangements. My mother, my sister, and I all slept in one twin-sized bunk bed that was just big enough to sleep a 5 foot, 8-year-old. The bunk bed set was missing the top bunk so we were forced to share the small bed frame on the bottom bunk. The bed consisted of a wooden frame that was covered with very little cotton padding with an elastic wrap on the bottom to hold it in place. Sleeping on the floor wasn't a better option because we had wooden floors and no extra comforters to create a pallet. And to top it off, for a long time we had mice that had infiltrated our space. We couldn't afford an exterminator so my grandpa would have to resort to the cheap fixes–mousetraps and peanut butter. While asleep, I would be awakened by the sound of mousetraps popping and snapping in the middle of the night. Then the next morning I would help him throw out the dead mice and reset the traps; out with the old, in with the new. This, of course, never completely solved the problem, but it temporarily helped cut down the night traffic of mice racing from room to room.

In addition, there were many times when my sister and I went to bed hungry. Our lights and water were shut off for extended periods of time, and the only light we had in our room was a cheap candle that burned out rather quickly. And when the candle burned out, all we had left was the illumination of the moon and the agony of our reality.

As I got older and the complexities of my life began to set in, I began to experience sleepless nights with tear-filled eyes as I lay in bed aching from the frustration. The tears symbolized the pain of growing up in poverty and the life of a young man with an absent father. On occasion, I would lay there and think about my father. I thought to myself, "I wonder where he is? What's he doing instead of being here with me?"

There were many nights where our situation would get the best of me. I cried tears to God asking him, "Why? Why us? WHY ARE YOU DOING THIS TO US?" And for years, I didn't understand why my life was made so difficult. I didn't understand why my father had to be addicted to crack. I didn't know why my father left me and why life was so hard for us and not everyone else. I didn't get it!

My mother would remind me all the time that things will get better one day. I would ask her about my dad, "Why doesn't he love me?"

And she would answer back, "Kris, he does. He loves you, but he's going through some things right now. He'll be back soon."

I had never heard him tell me that he loved me. Even though this was a difficult time, I had to hold onto the belief that what she was telling me was the truth. There were days where she would call him and put him on the phone with me. Right after I would say 'hello' I would hear the best phrase ever in life.

"Hey son, how you doing?"

I would immediately get excited inside hoping that this was THE day that my mother had been telling me about! This was the day that he would come back into my life!

"I'm good, are you coming over today?" I would ask.

"Nah, I'll be there tomorrow afternoon and then me and you can go hangout for a lil' while," he would say. And I would always respond back with an excited, "Okay!" For me, this was a big day to look forward to! I was so excited to hang out with my pops!

The tomorrow he spoke about would always arrive and I would always be extremely excited. I would be so anxious to get home from school to meet him. I would sit on the front steps of the house and wait patiently for him to get there. Some days I would sit on the porch steps and wait 30-40 minutes, other days an hour or longer waiting and knowing in my heart that he would keep his word to me and show up. Rain or shine, I waited as long as humanly possible. I didn't want to miss him if he pulled up and he didn't see me. When it rained, my grandmother would tell me, "Kris, it's raining come and sit inside the house and you can watch for him from the window." We had a picture window in the front of the house that overlooked the street. So if he pulled up I would see him before he saw me in the car he borrowed to pick me up.

Nine times out of ten I would sit there on the front steps of the house for hours, in the sun or the rain, and end up disappointed because he would never show up. And usually after this happened, I wouldn't hear from him for weeks and sometimes months. And when I did hear back from him I would never bring up being stood up and the heartache associated with it in our conversation. I would pretend as if it never happened. I quietly dealt with the disappointment. It haunted me for years as to why he'd do this to his son over and over again.

As a young boy my dad is the one I wanted to be like. This is who I wanted to walk like, talk like, and look like. So, the times he decided to keep his word I had to cherish and treat it like it was the last time I'd see him, because it felt like it could've been. I never knew when I was going to see him again. These experiences played such a critical role in our relationship because as I reached my teen years, his disappearing acts grew more frequent as my impatience grew stronger.

Through all of this I had to remember that it was not his fault. My father suffered from an addiction to crack. In the beginning, his addiction was the worst thing that could have ever happened to me. But at the same time, I look at his addiction as a sickness, similar to a disease like cancer. And just like cancer, there is no cure, only treatments. After 20+ years of drugs and alcohol, my father has been sober for a few years now. His fight for staying sober is a day-to-day process. This is something he will have to battle with for the rest of his life.

As a young man I didn't think of it this way. Now as an adult I have a better understanding as to why he wasn't there for me. I now understand that it was best for both of us! Because of my understanding this part of my struggle and the love I have for my father, I have accepted a new way of looking at my life. If he had been there for me growing up while he was on drugs, there's a good chance that I would have turned out to be just like him due to his fatherly influence and my surroundings.

Now, I may not be able to explain why certain things are happening in your life right now, but I do know this: they're happening for a reason that's beyond your level of understanding right now. And as you proceed on your journey you will begin to gain a clearer vision and discernment of it all. But the only way to get this is to keep fighting and refuse to give up! Your struggle will one day become a testimony and a word of encouragement for others to use as their armor during their battle.

So, it was necessary that I go through this struggle while on my journey. Remember that going through tough times is mandatory! There are no short-cuts or easy routes to your goals! For you to reach your dream you must create a new set of habits, beliefs, and self-disciplines that you've never had before! Motivational speaker Bo Bennett once said, "The discipline you learn and the character you build from setting and achieving a goal can be more valuable than the achievement of the goal itself." I say he is 100% correct!!

So while on your journey you may lose your car, you're lights may be shut off, you may be evicted from where you live, your phone might be cut off, and you might lose your job! You may even be diagnosed with a serious illness! All of these things have happened to me while on my journey. This is a part of the process! You must make it through this storm on your journey to prove to Life that you want this and more importantly, to become the better version of you! This new you will take you places in life that you never imagined going! This new person that you will become at the end of this journey will make it worth the fight.

Recap: Key Ingredient #4
THE STRUGGLE: STRUGGLING IS HEALTHY AND PART OF THE PROCESS!

While going through the struggle you will really find out what you're made of. You will face challenges and test that the average person would give up on. You must find the strength, courage, and support to keep fighting no matter what happens! You must develop a hunger so deep that the only thing that will be satisfying is the feeling you will have when you're dream becomes a reality. After making it through this stage you will have a defining moment in your life. This is the time where it will all come together and begin to make sense. And you will be forever thankful because of the person you have now become. And you will realize that it was worth it!

Chapter 5

IT'S HARD: IF IT WAS EASY, WE'D ALL BE SUCCESSFUL!

"Life's goal is to force you to give up on your dream. Life wants to see you quit before you do something great!"

Let's face it, going after your goals, reaching your dreams, or simply becoming a better you is not as easy as some people make it seem. Our current economic conditions, life in general, or maybe your past, is always getting in the way of you achieving your goals. As children, most of us had someone who told us things like, "You can be whatever you want in life." However, there's one thing that the adults in our lives failed to tell us. And that one thing they left out is: **It's Hard!**

I'll be the first to admit that living your dreams and reaching your goals is hard! It's not easy changing your behavior, adjusting your attitude, and facing your everyday obstacles. It's not easy finding the strength to keep going when no one believes in you. But I'm here to tell you that even though it's hard, there is still a way for you to win! And once you've survived the struggle you're still not out of the woods. Life is still going to take some last minute swings at you just to test you before reaching the finish line.

On April 10, 2010, I was in Oklahoma City, Oklahoma attending a business convention. During a break for lunch with a few business associates, I began to feel a funny, tingling sensation in the right cheek area of my face. My first thought was, "Wow, this cheeseburger sure is spicy." Everyone else kind of shared the same sentiment. So, I just ignored it and continued to finish my meal.

After lunch I went back to the convention center to attend the last of the breakout sessions that were happening that day. As the day went on this tingling sensation in my face intensified. I began to drink water, chew gum, massage my face, eat fruit, you name it! What's the significance of eating fruit? Well, growing up, we couldn't afford to go to the doctor, nor could we afford prescription medications, so one of my grandmother's home remedies for sickness was eating a piece of fruit.

When the convention was over for the day, a few of the guys wanted to go out and have a drink. I decided it was best I head back to my hotel room to call it a night. I wasn't feeling the greatest and I wanted to sleep off whatever was happening to my face. It was the last day of the convention. I woke up the next morning in my hotel room and I realized that the sensation in my cheek had gotten much worse overnight. I went to the bathroom and I took a look in the mirror. I realized that my face looked normal, but it didn't feel normal. There were no signs of pain, just an intense numbness. I began to convince myself that maybe it was something I ate or maybe I just slept wrong. Either way, I knew something wasn't right. So I grabbed some fruit to eat and began to head over to the convention center.

As I listened to one presenter after another, my face was getting worse. Then all of a sudden, one of my associates came to me and asked if I would deliver a 10 – 15 minute impromptu motivational speech to the audience. I agreed even though I wasn't feeling my best. I got up on stage and took the microphone with almost 100 pairs of eyes on me. They were looking for me to give them a few nuggets of wisdom to help them achieve their dreams and grow their businesses. As I began to speak, I noticed that I was having a difficult time making my mouth form the words that I wanted to say. I hurried through my speech the best that I could, struggling to pronounce even the simplest of words. I wondered if they were seeing what I was feeling, but at the end of my speech not only did I receive a warm round of applause, I also asked one of my business partners how I sounded and he gave me the assurances I needed.

I was still not sure what was wrong, but I could tell it was more serious than I thought. I prepared to head back home to Grand Rapids, Michigan. Fortunately, I wasn't alone on this drive. I made the long drive with a business partner who chartered a bus. While on the 16-hour drive home, I decided to take a nap and see how I felt when I woke up. After a few hours of sleep, I woke up and literally began the journey through one of the most traumatic experiences of my life.

There was no longer a tingle, the entire right side of my face was completely paralyzed! I was devastated! I couldn't figure out why or what had happened. Fear engulfed my entire mind and body and the weight of an uncertain future crushed my spirit.

My associates and I arrived at a rest stop and I went to get a bite to eat. I took my first bite and began to chew on only the left side of my mouth because I had no feeling on the right side. As I was chewing, I realized that I couldn't hold my mouth closed. Food began to fall out the right side of my mouth. I attempted to hold it in without using my hands and it didn't work. Now, I was more concerned than ever before! Not only did I not know what was wrong, but I also couldn't eat or drink! I was sitting with one of my associates and as I began to catch the fallen food particles with a napkin I mumbled, "Addis, something isn't right with my face."

He turned to look at me and said, "Whoa! Yeah, you're not looking to good. How do you feel?"

"I feel just fine overall, it's just I can't feel my face," I responded.

"Let me go and get someone to see if we can help you," he whispered to me.

"NO! Addis, don't tell anyone about this. I don't want to draw tons of unwanted attention to myself. I'll call my doctor and see him as soon as we get back to town," I told him.

On the outside I look strong and prideful. On the inside I was scared beyond what you can imagine.

As soon as I got back on the bus, I pulled out my cell phone and I began to research my symptoms. After a little reading about my symptoms my first thought was that I had had a stroke while I was asleep. I was able to move the rest of my body, but unable to move my face so that wasn't the correct diagnosis so I kept on searching.

Over 24 hours had passed since my symptoms first surfaced and now I was just arriving back in Grand Rapids. My wife, Chawntrell, picked me up and rushed me to see my doctor. My doctor took a look at me and after a few tests he diagnosed me with something called Bell's Palsy. I had never heard of this before and I wasn't sure what it was.

"Bell's Palsy is a disorder of the facial nerve that controls movement of the muscles in the face. And when this nerve is damaged, irritated, or swollen it causes pain and paralyzes the muscles in the affected side of the face," he explained.

I looked at my doctor and I asked, "Doc, how long is this going to last? Am I going to be ok?"

He looked at me and sighed. Then he responded, "Kris, it's kind of hard for me to say at this point. We can usually correct this type of problem in 2-3 weeks when it's been addressed in the first 24 hours of it happening. Since this started over 24 hours ago, I just can't say. You started with minor symptoms and now you're showing serious signs of paralysis. Honestly Kris, I just don't know what to say. It could last a few weeks, a few months, or even years. You could even be left with permanent damage for life. I just don't know at this point. All we can do is treat it and be patient."

These were not the words I wanted to hear. When I heard him say this, I watched my entire career as a speaker come to an immediate end. At that moment, I felt my stomach turn and my eyes began to water. I worked so hard to reach my dream and now I didn't know if I would ever be able to speak in front of an audience again. After all of the losses I had already had, this news was devastating. Having only been married for seven months, I was already thinking about how I was going to convince my wife to leave me because this was not what she signed up for—taking care of me was not part of the plan, not part of my plan.

She said, "Kris, remember when we got married?"

"Of course," I responded.

"This is for life," she said.

In the midst of all this pain, I actually felt some relief.

The bad news from the doctor's initial diagnosis was just the beginning of my problems. From there he sent me to see another doctor–an ENT (Ear, Nose, and Throat) Specialist who works specifically on things dealing with the face. I had to see this specialist 3-4 days a week for progress reports, hearing tests, vision tests, neurology tests, M.R.I. tests, and X-rays of my face. With every day that passed, my symptoms grew worse and my optimistic outlook was beginning to fade. After numerous tests, the specialist realized that I had lost 95.5% of the movement in the right side of my face. I lost hearing in my right ear. I lost vision and the ability to close my right eye. I lost my sense of taste and I lost my ability to smile. Growing up the hood, I learned the art of not smiling because smiling was considered a sign of weakness. I took smiling for granted and didn't appreciate the natural ability to do it. At this point in my life, I would have given anything to get that gift back.

After two weeks of dealing with this facial paralysis, I was told to come back in for another appointment. My wife was working, so I decided to go to this appointment alone. The nurse came out and greeted me with a kind, "Hello." She had gotten to know me pretty well since I had been visiting so regularly. She walked me back to my room and I sat there and wait for the specialist to come back around. After about five minutes, the specialist came in and greeted me. We began to discuss the lack of progress my face was showing. Eventually, he made the decision to increase my medication dosage in hopes that it would speed up the healing process.

And then he said, "Kris, I've got some more news for you."

"Ok, let me have it, Doc. I don't know if it can get any worse," I responded back.

"Kris, I noticed something strange when I took a look at your X-rays. You have two cysts in your face; one on each side of your cheekbone areas. Now, normally they're nothing to worry about, but my concern is that they may be cancerous."

"Did you say 'cancer'?" I asked.

"Yes, but don't worry. It may be something else. The only way to know for sure is to have another X-ray done to find out. You will need to come back for that X-ray in about 2-3 months. Right now there's no way for us to tell. We have to give it some time and see what happens," the specialist said.

I immediately felt my heart fall into my stomach. I've never faced anything like this before! This was hands-down my biggest challenge yet! I once heard motivational speaker Les Brown (who's also a two-time cancer survivor) say, "Cancer is the most feared word in 13 languages." And for me, this was true! I was nervous and scared, but I was also prepared for this fight.

It was at this point that I realized that I would need to draw on all of the tools that I had been speaking about in public and the tools that I have mentioned in this book. I knew that it was possible for me to overcome all of this. I knew that there were people out there that had overcome this facial paralysis before. And I also knew there were people out there who had overcome cancer as well. But I didn't know anyone who had overcome them both at the same time! So I figured, just like Roger Bannister became the first to overcome the four-minute mile, I may be the first to overcome this!

I would sit at home every day, on the couch–again– frustrated and miserable from the nine medications I was taking and from the pain that I was in. Some days the pain was worse than others. I communicated a lot through text and email. Any lengthy phone calls or conversations would cause excruciating pain throughout the right side of my face. My meals were very limited in variety. I was forced to eat things that didn't require a lot of chewing. Most days it was chicken noodle soup. I was also forced to drink from a straw. The lack of strength in my face wouldn't allow my mouth to grasp the rim of a cup. At night, I was forced to sleep with a liquid eye gel (similar to petroleum jelly) that I had to insert into my own eye. Because I couldn't close my right eye, the doctors were concerned with the air drying it out and causing a cataract to form or blindness to occur. That was not a viable option for me, so I had to sleep with an eye-patch on to shut out the light and protect my right eye.

Every morning when I woke up, I would sit up in bed and say a prayer asking God to heal me and give me understanding as to why this was happening. But somehow, in the midst of my prayer, it would turn to frustration because I wasn't getting an answer and I didn't understand.

"WHY ARE YOU DOING THIS? WHY ARE YOU PUTTING ME THROUGH THIS? HAS MY LIFE NOT BEEN HARD ENOUGH? YOU TOOK MY FATHER. YOU FORCED ME TO GROW UP IN POVERTY, NOW THIS? I NEED TO KNOW WHY?? WHY ME?"

After venting out my frustration to God, I would get out of bed and go to the bathroom and look at my face in the mirror. Each trip to the bathroom was the same–disappointing and no signs of progress.

Two months went by and I still hadn't told anyone about the cysts that were found in my face—not even my wife. I didn't want to alarm anyone unnecessarily and thought it would be best to handle it alone until I knew more. I was preparing for one of my many appointments with the ENT specialist to check my progress. While I was getting ready, I took a few minutes to sit down and review some of the specialist's notes that had been given to me. In his notes, he had written about the two cysts and that I would need an X-ray to figure out just how serious they were. I was reminded that I would need to come back within 2-3 months. I suddenly realized that I was right at the top of the timeframe that he spoke about. So, I gave him a call and spoke with his nurse about me coming back in for the X-rays. A few days later I received a letter in the mail from him explaining what he found and that I needed to be seen as soon as possible! I called and made an appointment for the X-rays that day, I left his notes on the couch, and I headed out for my follow-up with the specialist.

When I came back home from meeting with the specialist, my wife was sitting on the couch where I had left his notes. She had a very disturbed look on her face.

"What's wrong?" I asked.

"You never told me about this. You never said anything about how you might have cancer! Why didn't you tell me?" she asked.

It was at that moment that I realized that keeping secrets was not the right move. I grew up keeping my emotions bottled up and hidden inside. I didn't talk about my fears because it was sign of weakness, just like smiling. Besides, we hadn't even been married a year yet and I could see the stress she was under with everything else we had going on. I didn't want to make it worse by telling her about this. I had hoped that I could have this all addressed and cleared up before she found out. But, I realized that it was time to tell her the truth and trust her with my fears.

"Well, I don't have cancer. They found two cysts in my face and they're a little concerned about them and want to monitor them. If it is cancer they will address it with the proper treatments. And if it's not, they may still need to do surgery to repair the nerve in my face especially if I don't get feeling and movement back in the next few months," I told her.

After having the next set of X-rays done we were forced to stay patient until we got the results. Even though I was frustrated with God because of my lack of understanding, I continued to pray day and night asking God for healing! I fed my mind with positive messages and did my best to stay optimistic. I stayed at home every day while my wife, Chawntrell, was at work hoping for a positive report. The day finally came when we got the call we had been waiting for.

I was sitting at home, writing this book that you are currently reading, and my phone rang. I answered the phone and it was the nurse from the hospital.

"Hey Kris, how are you feeling?" she asked.

"As good as I can, knowing the circumstances," I responded.

"Well, we've had a chance to look over your x-ray and the specialist noticed that the two cysts that you had in your face are gone! Honestly, we can't explain this and we don't know how it happened so quickly! Most cases we see like this they either get bigger or they begin to shrink in size. But your case is different.

They just simply disappeared and we can't explain it," she said.

An incredible wave of relief came over me. I thanked her for the good news many times over! And as soon as I hung up the phone, I broke down into tears. I fell to my knees right where I stood and I began to thank God for his healing! I knew that if the doctors can't explain it then there's only one explanation–and that's the power of God! I was filled with so many emotions–Relief! Joy! Hope! Faith! One hurdle down, one more to go! Next up: overcoming the facial paralysis!

Before I knew it, days turned into weeks, and weeks turned into months. I was in the fight of my life! My health issues began to weigh heavily upon wife and I didn't know if I would ever be able to speak in front of a room of people again. I didn't know what was going to happen. What I did know was that drawing on all of the tools that I have been speaking about in public, using the tools that I have mentioned in this book, as well as applying positive reinforcement to my thoughts and continuing with prayer—were the keys to winning this battle! If it worked with the cysts in my face, it's got to work with this Bell's Palsy, too!

I continued to follow this routine and after seven long months of battling health issues, financial struggles, and stress on my marriage, I finally got the other call that I had been waiting for. The specialist called and notified me that during the last set of tests I took, he noticed that the movement in the right side of my face was beginning to come back. Things were finally going back to normal and in time I should have an almost complete, if not full, recovery!

After that call, everything began to slowly come back over the next few months. I regained my ability to close my right eye! I regained my ability to whistle! I was finally able to smile again! And for the first time in a long time–I was able to kiss my wife again!! And as I wrote this part of the book, even though I have not gained 100% control of my face back, I'm okay with that. I say that because there are some who are left with serious, permanent damage and others who never recover from this type of paralysis– and I am blessed to have the ability to continue to live my dream.

What I've learned is that anytime you go after your dream there's going to be a fight. You will be hit; you will be left with marks, and even a few bruises. As for me, I simply consider the residual facial damage I have as nothing more than a few marks and bruises. I came out victorious in this fight! I went in prepared to fight for my dream! I had to fight for my life! And if you're reading this book, you're one of the people I was fighting for–I had to fight for YOU!

You've probably faced some tough and trying times in your life. You've had some things happen that the average person would never make it through. And because you're still fighting, I know you're a WINNER!! I know that your victory is much closer than you think. And just like my story, you must keep fighting!! You must not give up! Use this as your **It's Possible** story! The truth of it is you're a winner! And you know that you're a winner! Winston Churchill once said, "The truth is incontrovertible, malice may attack it, ignorance may deride it, but in the end; there it is."

So I say to you, know your truth! Know that it's going to be hard, but you have what it takes! And I promise– you can win!!

***

Recap: Key Ingredient #5
It's Hard: If it was Easy, We'd all be Successful!

I never knew that for me to reach my dream I would have to face and go through true, life-changing ordeals. Remember, you must be prepared for the fight of your life if you truly want your dream! I could not allow that negative, little voice in my head to tell me that I would never be healed or that I couldn't win this fight! I had to find a way to drown him out! And I did this through prayer, positive thoughts, positive reinforcement, and positive support from my wife. Apply these things to your life and great things will come!

Chapter 6

YOU MUST HAVE FAITH: YOUR FAITH HAS A HUGE APPETITE!

"Temporary failure is the tool used by LIFE to discourage true champions from winning."

I am very proud of you!! You are almost there! You have fought tooth and nail and survived things that most people would have given up on a long time ago. You are on your way!

The next step on your journey is very important. I believe it to be the most important ingredient in this entire book. Without it you have no chance. I repeat—no chance of reaching the finish line! This ingredient will carry you when you feel you can't carry yourself and when you have nothing else left to give.

The sixth ingredient is: **You Must Have Faith!**

Biblical scripture says, *"Now faith is the substance of things hoped for, the evidence of things not seen. (Hebrews 11:1 NKJV)*

According to Webster Dictionary, Faith means, *"a firm belief in something for which there is no proof."*

Whether you know it or not, you have been standing on faith this whole time. Faith is what has brought you this far on your journey. When fear showed up and you felt the odds were against you, your faith brought you through. Remember when you were ready to quit and give up on this dream? Your faith kept you going when you didn't think you had anything left. Remember when your friends and family laughed at you? Remember when they told you that you were crazy for pursuing this dream? That's when your faith nudged you in the back and said, "Don't listen to them, just keep going." And don't forget about when you lost your job. Your faith stepped in and said, "Trust me. I'll give you back more than you just lost. Just keep pushing forward." You see, your faith has been your biggest supporter this whole time. It's brought you this far and as long as you continue to believe, your faith will continue to carry you to your dream.

Throughout this book, I have encouraged you to focus on your dream. My goal has been for you to consistently see yourself already achieving this goal–envisioning a mental picture of what it is that you want and believing that you can reach it–no matter what life throws at you. You have had faith in the words on these pages and the ingredients I have given you. You have followed them with the belief that, "If Kris can do it, I can do it!"

I'm not here to preach religion to you, but I personally believe that there is a Higher Power, much greater than you and I, that controls all of this for us. And without this Higher Power, our dreams are just a powerless figment of our imagination.

Without faith I would have given up on my dream a long time ago. My faith brought me through when I knew no one believed in me. Without faith, I would not have survived the extremes of poverty that I came from. Without my faith, I would not have survived my traumatic paralysis that once affected my face. And without my faith, this book would not exist.

Faith has played a major role in my life and in my success. And this is why I feel I must share it with you. I know that if it were not for my faith and my belief in God I would not have made it this far. I'm here to say that for you to make it on your journey you must have faith in a Power much greater than yourself!

Life can be very interesting at times. One moment things are going well in your life. You're making great progress and things are moving in the direction of your choosing. And then that dreadful unexpected day is going to come when life is going to attack you to see how bad you really want your dream. This is also the point on your journey when your faith will be truly tested! This is when there's nothing that anyone else can say or do to help see you through. There's nothing that your friends, family, pastor, teachers, mentors, advisors, or perfect strangers can say to you to help bring you through this part of your journey. All the motivation in the world won't help you during this time. And that is when You Must Have Faith and belief in a Power much greater than yourself to bring you through.

After working at the tuxedo store and working a few different sales positions, three friends and I decided to become partners and start a new marketing company. Our goal was to open a successful marketing agency that would have multiple locations around the country. We would market small businesses locally and even a few national chains. My goal was to one day move to Phoenix, Arizona where the weather was warm (more often than not) and my days of shoveling snow and freezing my butt off several months out the year would be over. Even though I had never been to Arizona before,

I was prepared to venture out and try something new. So, I thought that would be a great location to start a new business.

I didn't have much experience in business, except for a couple of years in an entry level marketing position, and I really felt that this may be the "door to opportunity" that I had been eager to walk through. It was the biggest decision I had ever made in my short life, and I felt like it was going to be even more than I had originally hoped it would be. This opportunity would help pluck me away from the inner city and plant me in a place both physically and mentally where I could grow. I knew that if I was willing to work extremely hard, that one day I would achieve my goal of becoming "successful!"

My partners and I decided to move to the east side of the state in Michigan and open our first location in Garden City. We agreed that this would be a great starting point and from there we would branch out to open another location in Phoenix.

We spent our first year in Garden City–homeless. We slept in different cheap motels for months. My partners and I shared one room and every night we would rotate our sleeping arrangements–two people sleeping on the beds one night while the other two slept on the floor. We used this living situation to sharpen our competitive edge and enhance our negotiating skills because the luxury of sleeping in a bed was given to the man who brought in the most business that day. When we were negligent in paying for our motel room, we'd strategically place our belongings around the room along with our bags so that the room looked as if we had every intention of staying another night and that we simply "forgot" to pay. On more than one occasion, we would come back to our room only to feel like Will Smith in the movie, The Pursuit of Happyness, because just like his character, we would find our bags sitting outside the motel room door. On nights like this, we would move on to the next cheap motel; some place where I could convince them to cut us a deal for the night. I knew that this part of my journey was not going to be easy, but I didn't expect to be periodically homeless and hungry.

During this period of time, there were days when business went well! It wasn't life-changing money, but it was enough to treat ourselves. We would splurge and have a hot meal at a chain restaurant. I didn't have money to eat like this often, but when I did, I felt like I was eating filet mignon from a five-star restaurant! And then there were the dreaded days where business didn't go as we had planned. On these days, we were stuck eating pre-packaged, unhealthy snacks from the gas station down the street.

After a few months of living like this, my family back in Grand Rapids began to think I was crazy! My mother said things like, "Kris, just come back home and find work here. It doesn't seem like this is working out for you. Maybe you can just get a job here that pays well." And I remember one of my cousins once told me, "Kris, you will never have a million dollars in the bank doing this!" Sound familiar? Ever have family and friends say these types of things to you?

After hearing these things from my family, I began to question myself. I remember one of our office rules was that we had to wear a suit jacket every day to work. And I remember showing up at the office in a cheap, blue suit that I bought at a thrift store for $12. It was the only suit that I owned. At one point, I wore that suit three days in a row. One of my partners came up to me and said, "Kris, why don't you buy a new suit? You can't keep wearing that one." I didn't have a response for him. Feeling a bit embarrassed, I just walked away and went into the bathroom. I looked into the mirror and I asked myself, "Can you do this? Do you really think that you can do this?" These two questions began to weigh heavily on my conscience. You see, my family was part of my motivation for doing this. I wanted to one day have enough money to be able to help them all! But it was hard to stay motivated each and every day, when I knew that my family didn't believe in me—nor did they believe in my dream. I had to remind myself that they just didn't understand. They didn't understand that this journey that I was on was bigger than where I was living, what kind of suit I wore, or what I was eating for dinner. I was doing this to fulfill a hunger on the inside!

After my first year of struggling with this business venture and with life, things began to get better! I finally had enough money to get an apartment and business was on the upswing so much that it was requiring us to travel across the Midwest! I was loving life and what I had accomplished up to this point! I felt all the struggle had been worth it! And then…BAM! Life blindsided me again. After working hard and reaping the benefits of that hard work, things started to take a turn for the worse. Our business began to slow down. We began losing money faster than we could make it!

I remember working a full day outside the office and when I got back I was told by one of my partners that we would be having a full staff meeting once everyone had arrived back at the office. After waiting for a while, all three of my partners showed up together. One of them got up and began to explain why he called this meeting.

"I called this meeting today because our business is not going in the direction that we would like to see it move. We have had huge success over the last year and now things are beginning to fall apart," he said.

From there, he went on to use an analogy about an apple pie. "A woman asked her husband to go out and pick apples for her so that she could make a fresh apple pie. The woman's husband went out with his ladder and climbed to the top of the tree where he knew the apples were the best! He pulled down 11 apples that he felt were suitable for this pie. When he got down he realized he was one apple short. His wife needed 12 apples to make her apple pie. He didn't feel like climbing all the way back up the tree for just one apple. So he just picked up an apple off the ground. And even though the apple had a few soft spots he didn't feel it was a big deal. So he used the rotten apple to complete his 12 apples," he said.

I sat there amongst my colleagues very confused because I didn't know where he was going with this story.

He continued, "When you make a good apple pie you must have all good apples to make it. If you have one bad apple it will ruin your entire pie. So I am going to read off a few names. And if I call your name, just stand up where you are."

I heard two names and then I heard, "Kris Mathis stand up."

"We have decided that you are the bad apple that is ruining our good apple pie. You are no longer a partner within our company. Please get your things and leave," he said.

I stood there in front of 20 people speechless. We were all speechless. No one saw this coming. I didn't say a word. I grabbed my things and I walked out to the hallway while the meeting continued without me. I didn't understand why this was happening! I had worked extremely hard to help build up this business and now I was being told that I'm not wanted there anymore! I just didn't get it! I waited patiently in the hallway, outside of the bullpen. I wanted to speak with who I thought were my partners and friends in this business to find out what was going on! After waiting for over an hour, one of them finally came out. He explained to me that the other two felt that they could grow the company without me and that they were not interested in meeting with me to discuss it. Their decision was final.

Long story short, I learned that I had allowed my excitement for this opportunity to cloud my judgment. I realized that due to my inexperience and impatience, I had signed paperwork that was not in my best interest–and there was nothing that I could do about it. I couldn't even open a new location on my own because of an agreement with our local merchandiser. I was forced to give up on this dream and everything that I had worked so hard for and move back to Grand Rapids, Michigan.

This is the point in my life when I moved back into my mother's basement. The only thing I owned was a couch and a T.V. I was so broken by my situation that I had given up all hope of ever trying again. I didn't believe that I had the strength to start over. And for the next four years I slept on my couch in front of my T.V.

I was sad, depressed, frustrated, defeated, and I felt that all hope was lost. I began to tell myself that maybe my family was right. Maybe I should go and find a job like everyone else. I had come to a point where all the motivation in the world could not help me. There was nothing that anyone could say to me to lift me out of this state of depression that I was drowning in so deeply.

Not only was I physically in the basement, but I was mentally in the basement as well. And I remember in my 4th year of living in this basement something happened that literally changed my life.

While I was asleep one night, on my couch, I had a dream. As my dream began, I saw myself preparing to go out on a stage and speak to a large audience of people. As I walked onto the stage, I saw bright lights and a mass of people that stretched back farther than I could see. I mean, there were thousands of people who had come to hear me speak. And when I walked onto the stage, the applause and cheers that I heard were like nothing that I had ever experienced before in my life. As I stood there, the crowd refused to stop applauding for me. It was obvious that I had something to say that they were looking forward to hearing. As the sound of the audience began to die down, I walked up to the microphone and as I began to speak, I suddenly woke up out of my dream. I don't know where I was, what I was there for, or what I was speaking about. All I know is that I had something that all those people needed to hear.

A few nights later, I was once again asleep on my couch and I heard a voice say to me, *"Kris, this is not what I designed you for."* I instantly woke up out of my sleep and sat up on the couch! I thought to myself, "Wait a second, he's right! This is NOT what I was designed for! I must give this another shot! I've got to try again!!"

I knew in my mind that this voice I heard was God reminding me of my true value and identity! I knew in my heart that life had dealt me a punch that was to finish me off! I felt like Rocky Balboa. In all the Rocky movies it didn't matter how bloody, bruised and beaten Rocky was, he kept getting back up! And towards the end, he would have a surge of energy, just enough to knock his opponent out and win the fight! And I decided that was going to be the same for me! I refused to stay on the mat or in my case, the couch! I had to get up and fight until I won!!

You see, during my 4-year stretch in my mother's basement, faith is all I had left. If it were not for my faith in God I would still be in that basement on my couch.

Some of you that are reading this book right now are physically and/or mentally "in the basement." You are sad, depressed, frustrated, and defeated. You have come to a point in your life where you have no idea how you are going to make it. Well, I'm going to say to you what I heard God say to me: ***"This is not what He designed you for."*** I once heard motivational speaker Les Brown say, "faith is the oil that takes the friction out of living." Remember, sticking to your faith will be the vehicle that will carry you through your tough and challenging times! Your faith has brought you this far! Don't give up on it just yet!! Keep fighting and you will be amazed at what your Faith will do for you next.

Recap: Key Ingredient #6
YOU MUST HAVE FAITH: YOUR FAITH HAS A HUGE APPETITE!

You must have faith in a Power much greater than yourself. There is going to come a time when all the motivation in the world can't help you. And this is when you will need to say, "Lord, whatever I face today, You and I can handle it. And I know, You will always make a way for me."

Chapter 7

THE VICTORY: 'TIS SO SWEET!

*"Even when the odds are against me
I'm convinced that I still have the
upper hand. I will not lose!"*

This next ingredient is the reason you have continued to read this book and continued to trust in this process. You gave yourself a **Reality Check** to see where you were in the pursuit of your dream. You learned to envision your "life's trailer" by going to your **Dream** Place. Next, you were able to see your dream when no one else could. Even when people told you "it" would never work, you still found a way to believe that **It's Possible** for you to reach your dream. Then, you bundled up to face

75

the nasty weather, criticism and comments that came during **The Struggle**. You knew it was going to be **Hard**, but you were prepared to keep fighting. And through all of this, you didn't lose your **Faith**. Now, here's the seventh ingredient.

The seventh ingredient is: **The Victory!**

This is one instance where the grass truly is greener on the other side! The Victory is the reason you have been fighting. I believe **The Victory** to be one of the sweetest parts of this process. This is when you get a chance to see all of your hard work, sacrifice, and discipline to begin to pay off. You actually cross the finish line and realize that it was worth all that you went through to achieve victory.

Frank Sinatra once said, "The best revenge is massive success!" This is the time to look at all those people who laughed at you, who didn't believe in you, and who told you to give up. With a peaceful smile, "I Did It!"

You knocked on the door to success because you were determined to become a **<u>Winner</u>**. And you kept knocking when others gave up. You knew that there was somebody home and you refused to quit knocking. And since you wouldn't give up, life was forced to let you in.

I have knocked on the door to success many times. And it took me almost 13 years of knocking before life opened it and let me in. Since then, I have achieved many victories on my journey to reach my dreams. I have overcome some of life's biggest setbacks while on my journey to becoming a **Winner.** I have endured tough times while growing up in the inner city. I have gone on to have a very successful career in marketing and I've been paid thousands of dollars to speak at live events. Most people would consider these tremendous achievements, and I would agree with them. I am very proud of what I've done, but I have one victory that I believe tops them all! This victory is one shared by my wife and I.

When I met my wife Chawntrell, she was a student at Grand Valley State University in Allendale, Michigan. My wife and I have considerably different backgrounds. Chawntrell grew up in Flint, Michigan, in a nice suburban part of town. And although she had some challenges growing up, they pale in comparison to the challenges that I faced growing up in the inner city of Grand Rapids.

Around the time we met, she was beginning to study Japanese. Chawntrell has always been fascinated with the Asian culture. I remember when we were dating she would always talk about how one day she would love to go to Japan. She told me she would like to spend a week there visiting the sites, tasting exotic foods, and, of course, participating in a little shopping. However, I had never thought about traveling that far! Again, just as I've shared in the beginning of this book, I would think to myself, "That's crazy! It's not possible for me to travel like that. Besides, international travel is expensive!" You see, I was no longer living in the inner city, but even though I was older and had learned a lot about positive thinking and positive thought processes, I would find it easy to revert back to the negative thought patterns I'd developed as a child, but only for a moment!

As our friendship progressed, so did my vision of what was possible for my life. We dated for three years and eventually got married on September 12, 2009. During that three year period, I never forgot that her dream was to one day go to Japan. I didn't know how I was going to do it or where the money was going to come from, but I told myself that one day I was going to take her to Japan. And there was nothing that was going to stop me from making her dream a reality. Three months after I made this commitment to myself, something amazing happened.

Chawntrell and I went out to dinner one night. While we were talking, I abruptly changed the subject. I grabbed her hand and while trying to control my excitement, I began to tell her how much she meant to me. I then slid a folded piece of paper across the table to her and I said, "This is for you."

She looked at me very puzzled and said, "Ok, what is it?"

I responded with, "Just open it."

She unfolded the paper and quickly realized that this was not an ordinary piece of paper. Then, without warning she shouts, "OH MY GOD!! I'M GOING TO TOKYO, JAPAN!!"

She was so excited that the vacation she dreamed about for years was finally going to happen! And I was extremely excited knowing that I could be part of making her dream a reality.

I had surprised the love of my life with exactly what she wanted—a seven day, six night stay at one of the nicest hotels in Tokyo, Japan. What made the trip even more romantic was that we celebrated our first wedding anniversary there. During our stay in Tokyo, we did whatever she wanted to do. We ate at all types of local restaurants, trying everything from fresh Sushi; to Octopus Spaghetti; to Grilled Eel. We visited everything from the Buddhist Temples; to the National Museum; to the Tokyo Zoo! And of course, she shopped at tons of local markets and gift shops! This was an experience that we will both remember for many years to come!

Some of you may be wondering why I consider this a victory. You see, for Chawntrell this was a dream vacation that she wanted for a long time. For me, this was literally a life-changing experience. Up to this point in my life, I had never dreamed about traveling around the world.

It was a victory for me because when you look at my life and know my story, according to society, I'm not supposed to be able to do this. I have truly beaten the odds and I have done things and been places that have, literally, amazed me.

This trip cost thousands of dollars. I don't say this to brag or to try to impress you; I say this to impress upon you the possibilities for your life if you simply commit to going after your dream! If it were not for my determination to reach my dream, I don't believe this trip would have ever happened for us.

Please understand, if you haven't reached your **Victory** yet and are fighting in **The Struggle** right now as you read this, know that I and many others have fought the same fight and have won! We have run the same race and crossed the finish line to receive **The Victory**. And let me be the first to tell you, IT'S WORTH IT!!

Now take a moment and envision your Dream Place. Think about **The Victory** and how it will feel when you have beaten the odds that you thought would crush you. Dream about waking up every day having a confident spirit because you're finally living! No longer are you settling for compulsory routines and tasks. You're energized by what you've accomplished and determined to continue your life's work. **Victory** is SWEET!!

Recap: Key Ingredient #7
THE VICTORY: 'TIS SO SWEET!

The Victory is the reason you have stuck in this race. You have kept fighting when most people gave up during **The Struggle**. And because you refused to quit, you now get a chance to see just how sweet things are as a **Winner**. Stay in the fight! What a day it will be when you can look yourself in the mirror and say, "I Did It!"

Chapter 8

SIGNIFICANCE: 'TIS SWEETER!

"I didn't begin this career to make millions. I did it to help millions."

$\mathcal{Y}$ou have now reached the final ingredient on your journey to your dream. You have worked very hard and fought through some of life's toughest challenges. You have reached your victory and enjoyed the success of becoming a **Winner**.

Now that you have achieved all of this, there is one more thing that you must do to truly separate yourself from the others. This last ingredient is something that I have found to be even sweeter than **The Victory!**

The eighth ingredient is: **Significance.**

Napoleon Hill once said, *"It is literally true that you can succeed best and quickest by helping others to succeed."*

Significance is something that very few find in life. I've learned that helping to change the lives of people through my own personal story is not done to make millions, but to help millions. I have taken on this challenge of helping people live their dreams by way of obligation. Yes, obligation, but not a burden. I believe that once we reach our goals and dreams, we are obligated to share with others how we did it. We must be willing to help others learn what we once did not know ourselves. It's only right that we shorten someone else's learning curve so that they may reach their dreams.

The feeling you have when you help someone reach their dreams is almost indescribable. The irony is that in giving your time and energy to help someone else get ahead, you receive so much more in return. It's a feeling that's beyond just being a **Winner**. It's a feeling of importance, goodwill, love, commitment, passion, and achievement.

I can recall many days and nights when there was no one around to help me realize the possibilities. My journey to success has not been easy, and many times, I was forced to walk this long road alone. Now that I have made it through the storm and become a **Winner,** why should I force someone else to go through it alone? I am obligated to share with others how I achieved my dream of a better life.

You see, there's someone out there right now that is reading this book and looking for a way to get what they want. And even though many people have given up on this person, they still refuse to give up on themselves. If I can help that person by way of my message, then I am fulfilling my obligation. My message is transmitted in many ways: speaking engagements, this book, motivational newsletters, my blog (*www.krismathis1. wordpress.com*), through personal coaching for people of all ages, and the list goes on!

I believe that the Bible scripture, "Ask and it will be given to you" (Matthew 7:7 NKJV) is very misunderstood! I believe that, yes, God will give, but He also expects you to do more than just ask. I feel we now live in a time where it's: "Give, and it will be given to you." I believe in the power of giving and sharing. A big part of my success is credited to my ability to give. My wife and I have made it our personal mission to touch as many lives as possible before we die. We contribute financially and also in ways that are not as tangible, but rather more impactful and valuable. We love to commit to helping people with our time.

I have a question for you. How would you like to be remembered? Do you want to be known as the person who achieved so much, but did so little? Or are you one who gave a lot and gained a lot more in return?

To truly be a **Winner,** you must be willing to do whatever it takes to make a positive impact in the lives of people. You must refuse to sit back and watch other **Contenders** consistently miss their mark! This is your chance to truly separate yourself from the pack!

When I made the decision to start speaking, I didn't do it with the intention of making a career out of it. I did it to contribute in a small way. Earlier I said, "Give and it will be given to you." I started by giving to my community. I wanted to help people of all ages, but I decided to start by helping who I consider the most important people in the world, and that's our youth.

In 2007, I started a project called *Teaching Kids Success.* My goal was to volunteer to speak with inner-city and at-risk youth ages 12-18. I wanted them to hear and see just how similar our stories really were. They needed to hear that I've had some of the same challenges that they face every day and they needed to see where I am now after surviving the extremes that I grew up in. I wanted them to know that if I could do it, they could do it!

I was eventually contacted to speak at schools, youth groups, etc. As I was being asked to speak, keep in mind that I'm of the mindset that I'm doing this to give back, not knowing that God had bigger plans for me. After months of giving back, life finally decided to open the door for success to come in and greet me. I began receiving media attention from numerous outlets including newspaper and T.V. The publicity turned out to be much more than I ever expected.

I was then contacted by a local high school. The administration believed in what I was doing and felt the authenticity of my message. They felt so strongly about their students needing to hear my message that they offered to compensate me for my time to convey it. We agreed that I would conduct small group workshops once a week for an entire school year. I never thought that one day someone would offer me money to do what I thought was just volunteer work. But I guess this is the power of giving back that opened these doors. After this experience, I realized that I was on to something special.

Since then, I have touched the lives of thousands of people throughout the United States of American and around the world! Every day I am amazed at how my message of success, dreams, goals, and overcoming adversity has spread around the world. I am repeatedly invited to be a keynote speaker for schools, non-profits, corporate functions, graduations, professional luncheons, disability advocate groups, churches, and the list goes on! Even though I have had success, I continue to volunteer by giving back my services once a month to a non-profit. I must stay true and grounded to how all this began for me.

I am so thankful for this opportunity to influence the lives of so many people. It has allowed me to fill a void within myself. You see, at one point in my life, I went to work every day with the sole purpose of chasing money. Then I realized that there was no real fulfillment and there was no finish line to indicate success that was based on monetary gain. Now, I go to work every day chasing **Significance**. I wake up every morning predicting how many people I can help. I prepare myself to be a leader who serves others and what I receive in return is an abundance of blessings.

Here are a few of the good people who have been touched by my message:

"I just wanted to tell you that a lot of what you said this morning helped me feel less lonely… Thank you so much for everything you shared today and for allowing me to share something that I have always been ashamed to talk about."

Sophia, Student

"You have a gift from God and you are using that gift to help others. Thank you for all you do to be an inspiration for others!"

Lynn Heemstra, Executive Director
Our Community's Children, Grand Rapids, MI.

"Kris, your message touches many, many, many facets of my life! I thank you for this word through your gifts! It is truly print and frame worthy! I AM closer than I think! Be prepared to welcome me on the "other side."

Katrina Couch, Grand Rapids, MI.

"Kris, thank you so much for coming. From everything I heard from students and staff you were the best opening Keynote we've had in the three years I've been planning this event. Thank you again and we'd love to have you back."
Paul Lichtenheld, Teacher/Event Coordinator Westfield
Community School, Algonquin, IL.

Comments like the ones you've just read keep me going! They have given my life a new purpose and meaning! This is why I believe that we are obligated to do more with our lives and not stop at just being happy with The Victory! There are people out there who need to hear how you've achieved your dream.

And in return for giving back, people will give back to you in ways unimaginable.

Recap: Key Ingredient #8
SIGNIFICANCE: 'TIS SWEETER!

The calling on your life is much greater than you know! You have an opportunity to do far more than just enjoy your own personal success. Anybody can do that! I believe to truly be a **Winner**; you must be willing to do more than just reach The Victory! It doesn't stop there! You must be willing to share your gift with the world! Once you do this, it will take you to a place of freedom, goodwill, and immeasurable happiness.

Afterword

"There's nothing special me. What
makes me different is my drive, desire
and dedication to be the best."

I recall making this statement to a large group of people early on in my career. Now when I read this quote I realize that I had it all wrong. I've realized that there is something special about me! I have more gifts than I'm giving myself credit for. I'm smart, talented, gifted in many areas, and I deserve the best that life has to offer! I told myself this everyday while on my journey to convince myself that I had what it takes to make my dreams a reality! And even though my past was not the greatest, I refuse to allow it to determine who I truly am!

Just like me, YOU have it all wrong! If no one has told you lately that there is something special about you, then let me be the first! You are smart, talented, gifted in many ways, and you deserve the best that life has to offer!! And even though your past may not have been the greatest you must refuse to allow it to determine who you truly are!

Now you know that for you to reach your dreams you must begin with a **Reality Check.** Then you will have **The Dream.** Once you begin to dream about what you want you will begin to see **It's Possible** for you to live your dreams. Next you will fight your way through **The Struggle.** And yes, it's going to be **Hard!** Easy is not an option! And **You Must Have Faith** to carry you when you feel you can't go on. And when you realize how important your faith is it will carry you over the finish line to your **Victory!** And last, once you begin to share with others how you achieved this dream, you will find something very few "successful people" ever find, and that's **Significance.**

Now that you have completed this book I want to leave you with one more piece of encouragement for your journey. It's a poem I wrote titled, **To Live Your Dreams.**

To Live Your Dreams

To live your dreams you have to be willing to fight for it,
make steps forward every day and night for it.
Be willing to give up time and sleep at night for it,
have patience, work hard, and do more than just try for it.
Remember, Martin had a dream and
he was willing to die for it.
You have to believe and have dreams at night about it,
feel your life is just useless and incomplete without it.
Be willing to take a setback to reach it,
and know that others before you have achieved it.
Know in your heart that you cannot be defeated.
Use all your strength, skills, and prepare to take action,
and not reaching your goal is never an option!
Stay moving forward towards your goal until you hit it,
and I promise through the power of God you'll get it.
THANK YOU.

ABOUT KRIS MATHIS

 **Kris Mathis** is a dynamic motivational speaker and author who has risen to international prominence by delivering a powerful and insightful message, which tells people how to shake off mediocrity and live their dreams today! Kris is repeatedly invited to speak for non-profits, high schools, colleges, company events, church congregations, graduations, and the list goes on!

Kris' words of motivation are published weekly in the Grand Rapids Times Newspaper, his Motivation for the Day Newsletter and Blog (*www.krismathis1.wordpress.com*). Plus he is the motivational voice every week on the Monica Sparks Radio Show.

Kris currently resides in his hometown of Grand Rapids, Michigan with his wife Chawntrell.

To book Kris Mathis visit www.krismathis.com and email your request or call 616-633-4939.

ABOUT SHANNON L. HARRIS

 **Shannon L. Harris** is a graduate of Florida A & M University where she earned a Bachelor of Science Degree in Journalism. She currently coordinates youth programs in civic engagement, leadership and employment for Our Community's Children, a public/private partnership between the City of Grand Rapids, Grand Rapids Public Schools and community partners in Grand Rapids, Michigan.

Shannon is also an accomplished dancer and choreographer for high school dance troupes to international retail trade shows. In addition, Shannon has written various radio commercials, newspaper articles, youth program curricula and she is a member of Delta Sigma Theta Sorority, Incorporated.

Shannon currently resides in Grand Rapids, Michigan.

To contact Shannon L. Harris, email her at shannonLharrisinquiry@gmail.com.